Have You Ever Noticed ?

Observations, thoughts
and comments
on everyday life...

By
Louis Perlin

Have You Ever Noticed

Have You Ever Noticed . . .
Copyright © Louis Perlin, 2007
All Rights Reserved

Williams Publishing Company
6176 Driver Road
Palm Springs, CA 92264

Library of Congress Control Number:
LCCN 2003116759
ISBN: 978-0-9666906-5-1

Cover Art by Karen Ross
All other art and design by Arte Moderno and Wild Beast Productions

Publisher's Cataloging-In-Publication Data
(Prepared by The Donohue Group, Inc.)

Perlin, Louis
    Have you ever noticed-- that people who leave the toilet seat up, never read books-- : a collection of observations, thoughts and comments on everyday life-- / by Louis Perlin.

    p. ; cm.

    ISBN: 978-0-9666906-5-1

1. American wit and humor. 2. Life--Humor. I. Title.
PN6165 .P47 2007
817/.6   2003116759
        Printed in The United States of America
                10 9 8 7 6 5 4 3 2

Without limiting the rights under copyright reserved above, no part of this book may be reproduced, stored in or introduced into a retrieval system, or transmitted, in any form or by any means, without permission in writing from the publisher, with the exception for the inclusion of brief quotations in a review.

About the Author

Louis Perlin was born in Massachusetts during the heart of the Great Depression, in 1931. He moved to Chicago and then to California arriving at the age of 16.

Lou's parents escaped from Russia during the pogroms with a little or no money, but worked very hard to give their children as best an education as possible. His father never went to school but when he died, at the age of 92, was able to read and write in several languages. So listening, observing and learning were well taught parental lessons for Lou.

Lou's greatest personal satisfaction comes from helping others whether in his business or professional life, or doing community service. For over ten years he visited high schools to talk to students about the real world of business experiences, the importance of getting an education, and the honor of community service.

For Lou, success is measured by the way you live your life. In business it's being professional and not doing things part way; with family (he has four children and 6 grandchildren) it's always being there and listening; in marriage it's being thankful for being lucky enough to have married Marilyn, now for over 35 years.

DEDICATION

To my wife, the love of my life, who constantly encourages me. It only took all of six hours to know that I would love her all of my life and that was over 35years ago.

To my daughter, Kerry Rose, who had a book on the best-seller list.

To our son, Dr. Bill Rose, also an author, and to our daughter, Margie Rose, who is a great screenwriter.

To our son Michael, who has served his country for over 24 years in the military.

To our six of our grandchildren whose accomplishments are over whelming and doing so at such young ages, makes us very proud.

To a dear friend, Paul Van Allott, who came from out of nowhere? Strangers can make a difference in ones life, if only people would be open to them. He proved that nothing is impossible.

Have You Ever Noticed

TABLE OF CONTENTS

ENTERTAINMENT	...	9
CHILDREN & PARENTING	...	33
DOCTORS & MECICINE	...	43
POLITICS & POLITICIANS	...	51
SPORTS	...	71
DINING OUT	...	75
CORPORATE LIFE & ADVERTISING		83
VACATION & TRAVEL	...	113
MEN – WOMEN; LOVE, MARRIAGE AND THE DIFFERENCES BETWEEN THE TWO		123
PEOPLE ARE PEOPLE	...	137
ABOUT REAL ESTATE	...	181
SOME LATE COMERS	...	187

… Have You Ever Noticed

Entertainment

Have you ever noticed ...

While waiting for the movie of Cole Porter's life to begin that just about everyone in the theater had white hair and when you mention his name to younger people they have a blank look on their face even though they know some of the music. On the other hand, I'm not certain who Justin Timberlake is!

Have you ever noticed ...

That some of the old time comics (like George Burns) just held a cigar and didn't light it up. They needed something to hold in their hands otherwise they wouldn't know what to do with their hands while performing.

Have you ever noticed ...

Family movies are now doing better at the box office than the shoot-em up type films?

Have you ever noticed ...

While playing a slot machine, and losing, the people on either side of you are winning and they sat down after you?

Have you ever noticed ...

Nudity in the films means that a woman can be seen totally nude and the only thing that a man shows is where he should be kicked?

Have you ever noticed ...

And wondered where your kids learned some of their language and then after hearing one of the CD's you know?

Have you ever noticed ...

Lately more and more entertainers are out promoting their favorite candidate, only to learn that some of them hadn't voted in 20 years?

Have you ever noticed ...

You can train a dog to do an awful lot of things except to use a litter box?

Have you ever noticed ...

In the past the big expense in going to the movies was the cost of the tickets, now it costs twice as much just for the popcorn, candy and drinks?

Have you ever noticed ...

In the movie the "Gladiator" that one of the horse handlers is wearing "Jeans"?

Have you ever noticed ...

Jack Nicholson's tie in the last scene of the movie, *"Few Good Men"*, when being escorted off by the MP's that his tie went from being on one side to being centered and he never touched the tie?

Have you ever noticed ...

In the TV movie, *"Pancho Villa As Himself"*, the scene when two men were carrying a "dead" person and they bumped into something, the "dead" man grabs his hat, but still tries to look dead?

Have you ever noticed ...

Movies that never make it to the big screen are shown on TV as Special Productions?

Have you ever noticed ...

Movies that critics don't like are usually loved by the general public? Remember "Happy Days?" Critics didn't like the show and it never won an award but was on the air for over 11 years

Have you ever noticed ...

That movie theaters now make you pay to see commercials before they show you the movie?

Have you ever noticed ...
That motion pictures that are "written by and directed by" the same person generally don't turn out to be a winner at the box office?

Have you ever noticed ...
Actors will say that they were ON-TV and IN the movies?

Have you ever noticed ...
Those video games your kids play are more violent than any movie, TV show you've ever seen, or any book you've ever read?

Have you ever noticed...

Banks will charge a fee on "insufficient funds" when they know that there is not enough money in the bank?

Have you ever noticed ...

That with over 100 TV stations available, there is often nothing that you can watch as a family?

Have you ever noticed ...

Trailers for new movies end up being more exciting than the actual feature?

Have you ever noticed ...
Most movies you see on cable TV have only one and two star ratings.

Have you ever noticed ...
You can tell someone that there's a billion stars and they'll never question you, yet say the paint is wet and they'll check to see for themselves?

Have you ever noticed ...
In Western's, cowboy's six shooters seldom, if ever, need to be reloaded?

Have you ever noticed ...
Those movie posters of a beautiful actress look different than when you see her in the movie? For some reason, the billboard figure looks better than the figure in the movie.

Have you ever noticed ...
Very few songs are being written about romance and love?

Have you ever noticed ...
In the movies a male actor can be isolated in some unknown place for a great number of days and still never need a shave?

Have you ever noticed ...

It's the actors and directors who make the real big money in the movie industry and the writers, who write the words, and come up with the ideas for the movie, are the least paid? I know, ask my daughter.

Have you ever noticed ...

Some artists never seem to achieve any recognition until after they die?

Have you ever noticed ...

How foolish some people act when they stand behind a TV news reporter who is broadcasting a report?

Have you ever noticed ...
Seeing someone fall, or slip or drop some messy thing on their clothes is not as funny in real life as it seems to be in a TV sit-com?

Have you ever noticed ...
That the motion pictures nominated for the Academy Awards always come out just before the awards are to be announced?

Have you ever noticed ...
That there is never a day that mattresses are not on sale?

Have you ever noticed ...
Hot dogs at a ballpark taste different than ones you eat at home?

Have you ever noticed ...
Disclaimers on TV are written so small and there are so many words, that even if you were given a full minute you couldn't read it, and you're given only two seconds at the end of the commercial?

Have you ever noticed ...
While watching a cooking show on TV how few times those TV chef's wash their hands when preparing all that food?

Have you ever noticed ...
After spending much time adjusting the sound on the TV to just where you want it, the commercial comes on and blasts you out of the room?

Have you ever noticed ...
Every so often a movie company will remake a classic movie and how seldom the remake looks as good as the original and even the historical facts change to fit the new directors ideas?

Have you ever noticed ...
The music we loved in the later 40's, and early 50's, was not that exciting to our parents? Isn't that the way we feel about our kid's music?

Have you ever noticed ...

All of the TV news reports stress crime, murder and fires with only the last minute on something that may be positive, and of a good nature?

Have you ever noticed ...

That no one really knows what the rating codes PG, G & R mean. Yet everyone including kids know what the "X" means?

Have you ever noticed ...

Some movies have so many four-letter words that if they were all removed; the movie would only be about three minutes long?

Have you ever noticed ...
That anyone over 50 years of age can't hear or understand the words of most new songs?

Have you ever noticed ...
Many people really enjoy opera but can't understand one single word being sung? Unless there are sub-titles.

Have you ever noticed ...
Those movies that have no violence, no sex, and no dirty words never seem to make money anymore? Exception, maybe a Disney animated movie.

Have you ever noticed ...
That Lenny Bruce would be considered mild compared to the comics of today?

Have you ever noticed ...
Every VCR or DVD jacket for just about every movie says that this is, "One of the best movies of the year"?

Have you ever noticed ...
So many of the children of people in the movie industry go into the same business, and really don't have the same talent? It's called nepotism!

Have you ever noticed ...
That some comedian's jokes get cleaner the larger their audience and the more famous they get?

Have you ever noticed ...
How many people go to a large stadium to see their favorite entertainer perform live, but end up being so far away that they can only see what's happening on a large TV screen?

Have you ever noticed ...
The new stadium-type movie theaters have so many steps that you're out of breath by the time you get to your seat and don't have time to recover before the kids say they have to go to the bathroom?

Have you ever noticed ...
That cable companies are giving us twice as many new programs, most of which are infomercials?

Have you ever noticed ...
Just about all women TV news reporters are young and (I must say) somewhat attractive and the men all look like they came out of GQ magazine?

Have you ever noticed ...
More and more actors are getting into politics and their speeches seem to be coming from some of their movies?

Have you ever noticed ...
Clowns never smile?

Have you ever noticed ...
The actor who played Charlie Chan was not Chinese?

Have you ever noticed ...
If you're in your 50's and you mention names of singers and movie stars of your era to a person in their 20's that the younger person will just stare at you?

Have you ever noticed ...
That women ballet dancers wear sheer costumes but the men dancers' costumes are more revealing?

Have you ever noticed ...
Since Clark Gable got by with saying 'damn" in "Gone With The Wind," it seems that every new movie has gone from "hell" or "damn" to words that got your mouth washed out with soap?

Have you ever noticed ...
Movies that cost $5 million dollars or less are making more money than movies that cost ten times that amount and are winning Academy Awards?

Have you ever noticed ...
Actors used to have a cigarette in their hands in just about every scene are no longer doing so and those that do seem to be dieing off?

Have you ever noticed ...
You can repeat a comedians joke word for word, yet it will never sound the same nor get the same response?

Have you ever noticed ...
That a blockbuster movie will be available on DVD within a very short time of being released in the theaters, will cost less to purchase than to watch in a theater, yet you still will go to the theater to see it?

Have you ever noticed ...

In western movies that the bad guy's teeth looked like they were just cleaned by a dentist and that he just had a manicure. If he's not wearing a shirt you'll note that he had shaved under his arms?

Have You Ever Noticed

Children & Parenting

Have you ever noticed ...

You will spend more money when shopping with your grandchildren then you do when you shop for them by yourself?

Have you ever noticed ...

While attending a Pop Warner Football game (or any other such sport for kids under 10 years of age) and you see one parent yelling instructions, is also the parent who never, ever gives time to be a regular coach for the team?

Have you ever noticed ...

When a child doesn't agree or do what their parents want, that the last recourse for the child is getting the grand-parent on their side and it always works?

Have you ever noticed ...
Upon giving a 1 or 2 year old child a toy that the very first thing they do is taste it?

Have you ever noticed ...
You would purchase a DVD of your grandchild appearing in a school play for $34.95, but would never consider paying that much for a regular VHS or DVD?

Have you ever noticed ...
When you have a single son or daughter over 30 years old, that it becomes everyone's obligation to get him or her married?

Have you ever noticed ...

Grandparents put up with things from their grandchildren that they would never have stood for from their own children?

Have you ever noticed ...

The terrible "two's" last for a minimum of three years?

Have you ever noticed ...

That you could put four one year olds (white, black, Hispanic and Asian) together in a playpen and that's exactly what they will do – PLAY?

Have you ever noticed ...

That the reason your kids play their music so loud is to drown out your screaming to lower the sound?

Have you ever noticed ...

Your children don't see any pictures when reading a book, yet you can see every event and hear every word?

Have you ever noticed ...

When a small child comes to your door to sell raffle tickets for some school charity or event that it's very difficult to say no?

Have you ever noticed ...
In England mothers never name their sons "Lou"?

Have you ever noticed ...
That kids working for their parents are expected to work three times harder then a regular employee?

Have you ever noticed ...
That people who get upset about children seeing nudity on TV rarely are bothered by the same nudity seen at the museum?

Have you ever noticed ...

That when your grandchildren puts their little arms around your neck they could have just about get anything they want?

Have you ever noticed ...

That younger people never ask or seek advice from their parents or grandparents? On the other hand, the parents and grandparents don't think they would follow their advice anyway.

Have you ever noticed ...

When a youngster has to go home early to practice his/her music lessons he/she wouldn't tell anyone why, but when a senior starts taking lessons they tell everyone?

Have you ever noticed ...
That parakeets and children have much in common? They often repeat words that you don't want them to and at times you don't expect, and neither really knows what they have said.

Have you ever noticed ...
Sitting in a restaurant a small child will act up, crying, making lots of noise and the parents just don't pay any attention, and everyone around them is hoping that they will leave soon?

Have you ever noticed ...
That some high school boys wear their pants so low that they embarrass plumbers?

Have you ever noticed ...
When a child is ready for school they're anxious to go and you wonder why in later years that they just don't continue to have the same excitement?

Have you ever noticed ...
When a child hugs you, it makes your body smile?

Have you ever noticed ...
That all babies are really beautiful?

Have you ever noticed ...
When asking a small child to keep a secret that they'll say "yes" and then proceed to tell the secret to a friend and ask them to keep it a secret?

Have you ever noticed ...
You're talking to friends about the good old days and how making a copy required that you use carbon paper and your kids ask what carbon paper is?

Have you ever noticed ...
At first you don't get upset when your kids are listening to rap music, but once you are able to understand the words being said, you pull the headset off your kid's head?

Doctors And Medicine

Have you ever noticed ...

You're on time for your doctor's appointment but must wait for at least a half hour? Then you're brought into another office where the assistant will take your blood pressure and temperature, then you wait another half hour before the doctor comes in and only sees you for a couple of minutes but charges for the full hour.

Have you ever noticed ...

That medicines advertised on TV make it sound like it's always the man's responsibility to be aroused and that there is no need for the woman to help?

Have you ever noticed ...

Doctors are never on time for your appointment, but should they need your services they expect you to always be on time?

Have you ever noticed ...
Doctors being interviewed on TV look like they just came out of Central Casting?

Have you ever noticed ...
Before a doctor will even see you, you must complete a questionnaire? Once in the doctor's office, he/she will ask you the same questions without even reading what you've already written on the questionnaire.

Have you ever noticed ...
That everyone becomes a doctor with remedies when you come to work with the sniffles?

Have you ever noticed ...
We know what Preparation H is, but the alphabet starts at A, so what's happened to those other Preparations?

Have you ever noticed ...
That insurance companies, when offering a new health plan, seem to be giving away the farm until they have a lot of subscribers and then start reducing the benefits until it's worse than the plan you gave up to join them?

Have you ever noticed ...
That when ill, and you see a doctor, your friends will strongly urge you to use their cure as being better than the doctor's?

Have you ever noticed ...

If you don't show up for a doctor's appointment you get charged, but if the doctor doesn't show then it's just too bad?

Have you ever noticed ...

When Congress talks about health insurance, they're really talking about improving their personal plan?

Have you ever noticed ...

How difficult it is to read a doctor's writing? Reason is, he/she can't spell the name of the medicine he/she's prescribing and hopes that the druggist knows what was written...and so do you.

Have you ever noticed ...
That you never see a muscle man or wrestler giving blood at the blood bank?

Have you ever noticed ...
That "Evian," spelled backwards is "Naïve." Is that how they get $2.00 bucks a bottle?

Have you ever noticed ...
That various medicines advertised on TV have so many side effects that you wonder if the cure is worth the risk?

Have you ever noticed ...

Having a doctor's appointment is just a waiting game? Never wait less than 45 minutes in the reception area, then 10 minutes in the examination room only to see the doctor for three minutes. You spend more time paying the bill than getting treated.

Have you ever noticed ...

That an attorney or realtor will immediately give you a business card upon first meeting them but a doctor doesn't?

Have you ever noticed ...

Weight clinics require that you buy their prepared food meals only to find that those prepackaged meals can be bought at the market for less?

Have you ever noticed ...

Most comments about Viagra come from men who say that their wives are happier, but how do they really know?

Have you ever noticed ...

Doctor's no longer make house calls and in case you are rushed to the hospital they won't go there either?

Have you ever noticed...

Medicines advertised on TV have a two-line disclaimer but when advertised in a magazine there's two pages of what to watch out for?

Have You Ever Noticed

Politics
And
Politicians

Have you ever noticed ...

When watching a congressional hearing and a congressman asks a question that it is more like a speech and you have difficulty understanding the question being asked? Worse yet, the person being asked the question will give an answer that no one understands and doesn't relate to the question being asked.

Have you ever noticed ...

No Senate Bill ever comes out of Congress as written? There is always "Pork" added. That's why a simple hammer for the military that normally would cost $3.00 ends up costing hundreds more. This way all Senators look good in their local area and the guy who really wanted to get the $3.00 hammer is clobbered.

Have you ever noticed ...

Talking politics with someone who hasn't voted, read the newspapers (other than the comics), or watches the news on TV is like trying to explain mathematics to a first grader?

Have you ever noticed ...

After the President meets with a foreign dignitary, he will always say – "We are happy to welcome our friend from such and such country," then proceeds to say – "We had a great conversation and have agreed on many things." This sounds OK until the dignitary gets home and he tells his people that they didn't agree on anything.

Have you ever noticed ...

Politicians running for Congress or the Senate always promise to improve education, more money for schools, more money for police and to improve our roads? Those are the same promises made since the Roman Empire and are certain to be made, again, in the future.

Have you ever noticed ...

At every local, state or national election there is one item on the ballot that by voting "NO" means "YES" or voting "YES" means "NO"?

Have you ever noticed ...
When you put "THE" and "IRS" together it spells "theirs"?

Have you ever noticed ...
Before Congress will pass a spending bill on a specific item, as it gets through Congress other congressmen will add on their own local "pork" expense, which has nothing to do with the original bill?

Have you ever noticed ...
How many people who love to speak publicly can put a whole room to sleep?

Have you ever noticed ...

When a governor is running for re-election he/she will go after the various unions for their support? And in order to get that support will pass legislation favorable to that union.

Have you ever noticed ...

Those countries fighting a revolution have plenty of money for guns and bullets but none for food or medical treatment?

Have you ever noticed ...

That the people who start wars never have any children of the age to fight in them?

Have you ever noticed ...

When something goes wrong with a government action the current President, Governor or Mayor always blames the problem on the previous administration?

Have you ever noticed ...

That political radio pundits rarely let their opposition finish a sentence on air and then complain that they have bias?

Have you ever noticed ...

That there would be no money for public education if the lottery were to be discontinued?

Have you ever noticed ...
That when a Senator talks about increasing jobs he really is speaking for his own district?

Have you ever noticed ...
How politicians talk when making a speech like they're talking to children. At the same time, making you feel like you don't understand what they're saying? Of course, most of them don't know what they're talking about, anyway.

Have you ever noticed ...
Many politicians enter office financially comfortable and when they leave office are <u>extremely</u> financially comfortable?

Have you ever noticed ...

when a politician, runs for office, he/she always promises to balance the budget, reduce crime, improve education and reduce taxes? At the same time the incumbent says, "I've reduced crime, balance the budget, improved education and reduced taxes."

Have you ever noticed ...

That a person with the weakest political argument is the one shouting the loudest to make their point?

Have you ever noticed ...

When a politician is asked a question they will never give a direct answer and then change the topic?

Have you ever noticed ...

After a person has served as a president of a charitable organization you never see them again at another meeting?

Have you ever noticed ...

That many bumper stickers say, "Proud to be American" or "These Colors Don't Run" yet the stickers are on a foreign built car?

Have you ever noticed ...

That people who complain most about government seldom, if ever, vote?

Have you ever noticed ...

Newspapers that favor one political party always have the good news about that party on page one, bad news on page eight and an explanation of the bad news in the editorial section? Bad news about the opposition party is always on page one and good news cut down to less than one paragraph by two inches, to be found ... somewhere near the classifieds.

Have you ever noticed ...

Employees work habits are different when the boss is not there?

Have you ever noticed ...

That so many products are marked "New" and "Improved", yet no one can tell the difference from the old?

Have you ever noticed ...

That when you pay for a house repair in advance that you wait a much longer time for the work to be done than if you paid when the work was completed?

Have you ever noticed ...

That "Barber Shops" no longer go by that name, now it's "Hair Stylist", yet you still feel and smell like you came out of a "Barber Shop"?

Have you ever noticed ...

When talking about the IRS you start to think of them as being in another form of collection business?

Have you ever noticed ...
Some people equate going to the office for 40 hours a week with working 40 hours a week?

Have you ever noticed ...
How many people's names often sound like their profession? For example: Raines (Weatherman), Hans (Landscaping), Glasstone (Brick Layer)? Baker (pastry chef)? How many do you know?

Have you ever noticed ...
How soon after retirement a person dies?

Have you ever noticed ...

Calling the electric company is no longer an easy task as you are answered by a recording in English; then repeated in Spanish and finally you are given a lecture on conservation. By the time you finally get to speak to a real person, you forgot why you called?

Have you ever noticed ...

That no matter how nice the boss may be talking to you, it still feels like something else?

Have you ever noticed ...

That since markets no longer give out Blue Chip Stamps they now have you join their "club" in order to get market discounts? All the time, hoping you don't use the card so they'll have a better mark-up on the goods?

Have you ever noticed ...
The boss says that he/she doesn't want any "yes" men around him/her and then proceeds to find out if everyone agrees with him?

Have you ever noticed ...
In California it costs more to run an electric car than one with a gas engine?

Have you ever noticed ...
When having a dispute with a utility company and they advise you to hold up payment until they review the meters, you then get a "past due" notice?

Have you ever noticed ...

Companies that advertise vitamins and weight reducing pills over the radio will always say that for the same price they, "would double the offer – as long as supplies last," and they've been running the same commercials for over a year?

Have you ever noticed ...

A gardener assures his income by first charging you to put fertilizer on your lawn and charges again to cut the grass, and then repeats the plan at least twice a year?

Have you ever noticed ...

That cars are getting more difficult to repair and service companies must now use computers to find out what's wrong? Then, proceed to charge you more for the computer analysis than for the actual repair of the car?

Have you ever noticed ...
That after you finally get your new employee trained, they move on to another job?

Have you ever noticed ...
When you're really busy, a fellow worker who may need to talk will come into your office and ask, "Are you busy?"

Have you ever noticed ...
Companies that are attempting to sell you products via the mail offer special programs like "mail-in" rebates? Question is, since they are already selling the product via mail why would you need to apply for a "mail-in" rebate? Question comes as a result of mail offer being made by Dell Computers, January 2005.

Have you ever noticed ...

After studying and getting your license, that none of the questions you needed to get correct in your test ever come up in the work place?

Have you ever noticed ...

When a Realtor advertises a house as being cute, or that it's a dollhouse, that it is also small?

Have you ever noticed ...

Cars that we owned 20 years ago look much better to us today and cost more now then they did then?

Have you ever noticed ...

How upset clerks get when you interrupt them to ask a question? Especially when it's two sales clerks talking to each other and they get upset when you ask where to find something?

Have you ever noticed ...

That some lawyers can charge you for 24 hours of work and you only spent one hour in their office?

Have you ever noticed ...

That the discounted computer you bought last week has gone on sale for 20% less than you paid for it?

Have you ever noticed ...
You really can't get any directions from a gas station attendant any more?

Have you ever noticed ...
When a salesperson says, "Don't worry about it", that you immediately start worrying?

Have You Ever Noticed

Have You Ever Noticed

Sports

Have you ever noticed ...

Baseball players are supposed to be role models but actually act more like children when the umpire rules against them?

Have you ever noticed ...

That baseball pitchers, upon being given a new ball, would rub and twist the ball yet no one knows why?

Have you ever noticed ...

That many basketball players earn so much money from various shoe sponsors that you begin to realize why the shoes cost so much? It's certainly not from the salaries they pay workers in those foreign countries.

Have you ever noticed ...
That runners are just about always by themselves?

Have you ever noticed ...
That as new professional basketball players are hired that they are taller then those that have left the game, yet the basket never seems to be raised? Only thing raised is the player's salaries.

Have you ever noticed ...
That you can't cry while under water?

Have you ever noticed ...
Tiger Woods never drives that Buick only uses it to carry golf balls and tees? He likes the car enough to give the keys to a stranger?

Have you ever noticed ...
When professional athletes, like baseball, hockey and basketball players, etc., lose a game they always say that, "they just couldn't put it together," or "we just were not up to the game today", or lots of other reasons, never once do you hear them say that the other team was better?

Have you ever noticed...
That we've been told that people evolved from apes, if so, why are there still apes?

Have You Ever Noticed

Dinning Out

Have you ever noticed ...
That after arriving at the new restaurant, where you made 6 PM dinner reservations, that the early bird dinner ended at 6PM?

Have you ever noticed ...
That the difference between an expensive restaurant and an average eatery is that the expensive restaurant gives you less food but charges more?

Have you ever noticed ...
You go into a restaurant knowing it's time to eat something but you're not very hungry, but once the food comes you really get hungry?

Have you ever noticed ...

When the waitress asks if you want mayo on your corned beef sandwich, you know you're not in a kosher deli?

Have you ever noticed ...

A waitress at a kosher deli will almost always say, "What can I get you hon"?

Have you ever noticed ...

While sitting in a restaurant and you see a couple together – one is reading and the other is just staring at nothing, you wonder, why they're together?

Have you ever noticed ...
That home cooking often really wasn't that great?

Have you ever noticed ...
At some of the really fancy restaurants the waiters act like we should be serving them?

Have you ever noticed ...
A senior meal, although less expensive, also contains about 50% less food?

Have you ever noticed ...

The bottle of wine you pay $35.00 for in a restaurant can be purchased for $6.95 at Costco?

Have you ever noticed ...

You could be the only person waiting to be seated in a restaurant and the hostess will always ask you, "How many?"

Have you ever noticed ...

How fast the waiter leaves after bringing you water and before you can ask a question, they're gone and then it takes forever to get their attention again?

Have you ever noticed ...

The dinner your mother made tasted much better than when someone else makes it using the same recipe?

Have you ever noticed ...

When a waitress asks if you want lettuce and tomato on your corn beef sandwich that you can bet she's not Jewish?

Have you ever noticed ...

That bacon tastes better when you pick it up with your fingers?

Have you ever noticed ...

That when dining in an expensive restaurant the lights are very dark and you have difficulty reading the prices on the menu?

Have you ever noticed ...

When asking your wife (or husband or friend) where they would like to go for dinner, they will respond, "anywhere you want", but when you choose, they don't want to go there?

Have you ever noticed ...

That some restaurants put so much food on your plate that it would be near impossible for one person to eat it all, so why do they want to charge you extra if you share a plate? If you don't eat it all they'll only have to throw the uneaten food away or package it for you to take home, which is about the same cost for the extra plate.

Have you ever noticed ...

That most restaurants give you "oyster" crackers with Clam Chowder soup? So why isn't it called "Clam" crackers?

Corporate Life And Advertising

Have you ever noticed ...

That you really feel in trouble when the mechanic asks, "who worked on this car before?"

Have you ever noticed ...

That coal companies are now claiming that their product is now the "clean" fuel?

Have you ever noticed ...

Major companies have computer answering systems that first come on in English and repeat in Spanish, then you have a series of keys to punch, after 10 minutes, you may finally speak to a real person who listens to your problem, says, "let me put you on hold for a minute", and then you get disconnected?

Have you ever noticed ...

When looking to purchase a fabric softener, the containers are all about the same size but the measuring cups are different sizes and you wonder which really does 60 loads?

Have you ever noticed ...

How often after filling up your gas tank, the very next gas station you pass has gas for less?

Have you ever noticed ...

Kitchen gadgets that are supposed to make your life much easier in the kitchen never really work as they do in the commercials?

Have you ever noticed ...

Every time you get in the 15 items or less line at the grocery store the person in front of you has more than the allotted items?

Have you ever noticed ...

That very seldom a person will quit a job over money? Generally it's over someone else in the office, or the boss said something that was not complimentary, or because they didn't get credit for a job well done.

Have you ever noticed ...

That once you buy something from a TV ad you can never ever get your name off the mailing list?

Have you ever noticed ...

That many orange, lemon and grapefruit drinks do not contain any real orange, lemon or grapefruit?

Have you ever noticed ...

How often a company's motto is "We are here for you" – you most often get a recording when you call?

Have you ever noticed ...

That the containers of food, cans and cartons remain the same size, but the quantity has been reduced, and the price remains the same?

Have you ever noticed ...

It's only on the day that you have to be at the office an hour early that you forgot to set the alarm and oversleep?

Have you ever noticed ...

Airlines are advertising that they are now giving passengers more legroom, but it's only a couple of inches?

Have you ever noticed ...

That large companies will fire people because of the bottom line profit, and then state that they are improving customer service?

Have you ever noticed ...

The commercials for frozen dinners look much larger than the ones you are able to find and purchase at the market?

Have you ever noticed ...

The reason that Fed Ex and UPS haven't merged is because they would be known as "Fed UP?"

Have you ever noticed ...

The companies that sell bottle water advertise that the bottles do not contain any carbs?

Have you ever noticed ...

That as soon as you are comfortable with new government or business forms – they change completely?

Have you ever noticed ...

We were told that coffee we enjoyed was no longer good for us, than we were told that it was OK to drink coffee, and again later we were told that it might not be a good idea, and now it's OK to drink coffee? Do you wonder if all this was created to establish a black market for the stuff?

Have you ever noticed ...

That no matter how many different types of toothpaste you use your teeth just don't look as good as the ones in the commercials?

Have you ever noticed ...

That you bought an appliance because you thought it was better than another only to find out that the same company makes them for both companies under different names?

Have you ever noticed ...

How in local car TV commercials the announcer is always yelling at you? Not because you can hear them better, but it's their way of pounding their message into your brain?

Have you ever noticed ...

If you're over 60, that the cost of a new car, even the least expensive one, is more expensive than your first house?

Have you ever noticed ...
That many sales managers can't sell worth a darn?

Have you ever noticed ...
That some water bottlers advertise that their water has no calories – did water ever have calories?

Have you ever noticed...
We press harder on the remote control when we know that the batteries are dieing?

Have you ever noticed ...

That in the past when you said "service" it was what the merchant gave you, now it's what you have to do to get anything from the merchant?

Have you ever noticed ...

People that need instructions are the same people that don't think they need them?

Have you ever noticed ...

Some people would never think twice about asking you to reduce your commission but would be greatly upset if you asked them to do the same thing?

Have you ever noticed ...
That tobacco CEO's are never seen smoking?

Have you ever noticed ...
That when you check into a hotel they call you a guest, but make you pay anyway?

Have you ever noticed ...
When a major company is caught having done something wrong, management always says that they don't know how such a thing could have happened and will look into it?

Have you ever noticed ...

People who promise to call an auto salesman or a Realtor® back seldom ever do?

Have you ever noticed ...

When Ed McMahon or Alex Trebek says, "it's only $3.69 per unit", they never says what a unit is?

Have you ever noticed ...

When children, in TV commercials speak that it's hard to understand just what they are saying ... exception is when they say UMMM?

Have you ever noticed ...

Some department or chain stores run so many sales that you really don't pay much attention to them anymore?

Have you ever noticed ...

You are told that a report is needed immediately so you work through your lunch hour, don't even go to the bathroom or take any breaks and finally get it done, only to be told that it wasn't really needed for a couple more days?

Have you ever noticed ...

When the street repairs are being made that there are more people directing traffic and giving instructions then there are workers making the repairs?

Have you ever noticed ...

That food products use artificial lemon and dishwasher products use real lemon?

Have you ever noticed ...

That the same people who get upset with you if you're not working hard, get even more upset if you're working too hard in fear of showing them up?

Have you ever noticed ...

Retirement packages given to CEO's of major companies are more than you (and I) will make in our lifetime?

Have you ever noticed ...

How little interest you get from your bank? They charge you if you make too many teller deposits, charge you if you don't maintain a certain balance, give you loans only if you really don't need the money, and give credit cards to people who can't afford them – and worse yet, they don't give toasters anymore?

Have you ever noticed ...

When business is bad, employees are fired, but the CEO still receives his annual Million Dollar bonus?

Have you ever noticed ...

That diet plans advertised on TV always has a disclaimer that says "Results Not Typical"? Does this mean that what we are seeing is not the truth, part truth or just an outright lie?

Have you ever noticed ...

When you give someone specific instructions and they follow those specific instructions that you are surprised?

Have you ever noticed ...

That most magazines have as many, if not more, pages devoted to advertising as they do to stories or features?

Have you ever noticed ...

Those post cards that are stuffed into magazines fall out when the magazine is opened and you just pick them up throw them away without reading them? The post cards that are attached in the magazine are also ripped out and also thrown away without reading them.

Have you ever noticed ...

Even when you're making more money that you still feel as broke as before?

Have you ever noticed ...

When auto dealers are clearing out their current new car inventory in anticipation of next year's models, that their advertising always says, "You'll never see prices like this again", meaning that the new models are going to cost more?

Have you ever noticed ...

Everyone thinks the other person's job is easier than his or hers?

Have you ever noticed ...
Old Realtors® never die they just become listless?
(Contributed by Nana Newman)

Have you ever noticed ...
Just about all clothing is on sale; therefore the sale price is actually the retail price, so you have to wait for another 25% discount before it really becomes a sale item?

Have you ever noticed ...
Soap is supposed to be 99/100% pure, but pure of what?

Have you ever noticed...
No matter what color bubble bath you use the bubbles are always white?

Have you ever noticed ...
That you can proof read a letter, newspaper ad or flyer and not notice any errors until after it's been printed?

Have you ever noticed ...
Road repairs don't start until traffic gets heavy and stops when there are few cars using the road? Then they put up orange cones narrowing the traffic lanes to one, and don't do any more work for several days?

Have you ever noticed ...
That the food never looks the same as it does on the carton or can?

Have you ever noticed ...
You planned your vacation for nearly a year, let everyone in the office know the date you would be leaving, and just a day or two before leaving, people you thought would be filling in for you advise that they, too, will be on vacation at the same time.

Have you ever noticed ...
When often asking an employee to do something the immediate answer is that "it's not my job"?

Have you ever noticed ...
People will work harder when they know it's a team effort, and not one person is getting the credit?

Have you ever noticed ...
That liquid soap doesn't foam like bar soap?

Have you ever noticed ...
The quietest person in the workplace does the most work and gets the least amount of attention?

Have you ever noticed ...
Going on strike might be the only way to get management to listen to your concerns, but it will take years to make up the loss of being on strike even if the demands are finally met?

Have you ever noticed ...
The large number of workers on a job, and still wonder why it takes so long to complete the job?

Have you ever noticed ...
Warranties on appliances, cars, etc., always seem to expire a week before or after you need service?

Have you ever noticed ...

When you're really busy, a fellow worker who may need to talk will come into your office and ask, "Are you busy?"

Have you ever noticed ...

After studying and getting your license, that none of the questions you needed to get correct in your test ever come up in the work place?

Have you ever noticed ...

When a Realtor® advertises a house as being cute, or a dollhouse, you find that it is also small?

Have you ever noticed ...
That after you finally get your new employees trained, they quit?

Have you ever noticed...
In the winter we keep the house as warm as it was in the summer and then we complain about the cost of heating the place and how warm it is?

Have you ever noticed ...
Cars that we owned 20 years ago look much better to us today and cost more now then they did then?

Have you ever noticed ...

That some lawyers can charge you for 24 hours of work and you only spent one hour in their office?

Have you ever noticed ...

How upset people get when you interrupt them to ask a question? Especially when it's two sales clerks talking to each other and they get upset when you ask where to find something.

Have you ever noticed ...

Companies that are attempting to sell you products via the mail offer special programs like "mail-in" rebates. Question is, since they are already selling the product via mail why would you need to apply for a "mail-in" rebate? (Question comes as result of mail offer being made by Dell Computers, January 2005)

Have you ever noticed ...

You really can't get any directions from a gas station attendant any more? Reason? They don't speak English!

Have you ever noticed ...

When a salesperson says, "don't worry about it", that you immediately start worrying about it?

Have you ever noticed ...

Flowers sold in a super market always look great and could stay in the market showcase forever, yet the minute you get those flowers home they begin to dry up?

Have you ever noticed ...

That many super markets require that you have a market card in order to obtain a slightly lower price. Virtually everyone has a card for the lower price, so why have the card in the first place? Wouldn't it be simpler and cheaper just to lower the prices and eliminate the need for another card in your wallet? It would certainly make the customer feel better.

Have you ever noticed...

When in the supermarket and someone rams your ankle with a shopping cart then apologizes for doing so, you say "that's OK?" What you really wanted to say was, "That hurt, you stupid idiot!"

Have you ever noticed ...

One of the best-known commercial slogan was, "I'd walk a mile for a Camel," and today if you had to walk to get it, you wouldn't?

Have you ever noticed ...
People say that you can save money by using the internet to send letters and for paying bills rather than mailing? Which maybe true except I probably never used $49.95 per month in stamps.

Have you ever noticed ...
As kids we didn't have iPods, computers, play stations or 200 plus TV stations to watch; yet we had as much, if not more fun, playing with our friends?

Have you ever noticed ...
Whenever there's a shoe sale there's never any shoes your size included in the sale?

Have you ever noticed ...

Upon receiving a fashion catalog from a large chain store, the styles are just what you had in mind. But, at the bottom of each page it reads, "Not available at all stores," and sure enough what you want is not available at your local store?

Have you ever noticed ...

When the daughter asked dad for money to purchase a pair of designer jeans, that her dad immediately ran to look up the company on the internet. If everyone ran to their computer to purchase stock for clothing that their daughter wanted to wear that the stock would become over valued and certainly would be speculative?

Have you ever noticed ...

Due to all the advertising of children's toys, if you give a child something other then what was being advertised, they don't want it?

Vacations And Travel

Have you ever noticed ...
That after traveling you're always happy to get home and to your own bed?

Have you ever noticed ...
How often you have packed for a vacation only to get there and find that you brought all the wrong clothes?

Have you ever noticed ...
That women who wear clothing up to their necks in the U.S., when in Tahiti they forget where their necks are?

Have you ever noticed...
When men are driving to a never before visited place that his wife will say he's going the wrong way? And she is usually right!

Have you ever noticed ...
That airlines claim that they are losing money yet you can never get a seat on a plane?

Have you ever noticed ...
That it's not until after you have your car washed that birds find a nice landing place?

Have you ever noticed …

That some commercial airline pilots leave the cockpit looking more refreshed than you do, and you wonder if they slept the entire trip?

Have you ever noticed …

That hotels call people who stay with them "guests", but make them pay anyway?

Have you ever noticed …

That cab drivers who most often are immigrants, can hardly speak the language, are the ones who know exactly where to take us?

Have you ever noticed ...

Some commercial pilots come on the speaker system to tell you how they expect the flight to go and "with a little luck, we'll be on time?" If I knew that the pilot was flying on luck, I would have waited for one that flew with skill. (contributed by, William Selwyn)

Have you ever noticed ...

Some people will check out a hotel room to make certain it's sparkling clean, but you wouldn't dare drink out of a glass in their "sparkling" home?

Have you ever noticed ...

How people on a cruise ship line up and rush for each meal as if it were their last?

Have you ever noticed ...

That "red caps" at airports don't actually wear a red cap?

Have you ever noticed ...

That bread tastes differently in different parts of the country?

Have you ever noticed ...

While on a vacation that if you don't mark your towels you might end up with the same ones used earlier?

Have you ever noticed ...
The only time you really get extremely busy and rushed to get things done is just before going on vacation?

Have you ever noticed ...
Airlines constantly complain of losing billions of dollars yet they still stay in business and you wonder how they do it?

Have you ever noticed ...
People who drive big SUV's swallow hard when putting gas in their vehicle?

Have you ever noticed ...

The price of a cruise is really inexpensive, but all of the charges for excursions, tours, drinks and bingo will cost more than the trip itself?

Have you ever noticed ...

The only time you catch a cold is before leaving on vacation?

Have you ever noticed ...

While on vacation you sometimes worry about what's happening at your job and upon returning learn that everybody did very well without you?

Have you ever noticed ...
It always rains the most when you are on vacation?

Have you ever noticed ...
People will say that, "I'm going to spend my two-week vacation just sleeping, eating and reading," but after a few days they're antsy and want to do something or go somewhere?

Have you ever noticed ...
When on a cruise you eat like you've never had food before and wonder why you've gained weight?

Have you ever noticed ...
When you get home from vacation, you are more tired and stressed then when you left?

Have you ever noticed ...
There are never any flies in the yard until you decide to stretch out on the lounge and take a nap?

Men – Women Love, Marriage And The Differences Between The Two

Have you ever noticed...

Before a man marries he will open a door for his date, place a napkin on her lap and (maybe) bring her flowers once in a while. After he marries, he walks in front of her, never opens the door for her, never places a napkin on her lap, leaves the toilet seat up and the only flower she gets is called "Pillsbury?"

Have you ever noticed ...

That those nice things you did for your wife before you got married and still do today is more important to her than any gift you may give her at any other time?

Have you ever noticed ...

A lot of men say they wear a size 34 belt, but the belt is under their stomach?

Have you ever noticed ...

That bathing suits are getting so small you wonder why some even bother to put them on at all? And the people you would like to see on a nude beach are never the ones that are there?

Have you ever noticed ...

Men claim to be the strongest of the sexes, but then again they never gave birth to a baby?

Have you ever noticed ...

That women are not deterred from dying their hair blonde even with the constant telling of "dumb blonde" jokes?

Have you ever noticed …
The person you thought you knew before getting married is much different after marriage?

Have you ever noticed …
That men may wear the pants in a family but the wife makes the decisions?

Have you ever noticed …
After years of marriage a woman will say, "It took years to train him to be as he is today," – in some cases that's not so good?

Have you ever noticed...

You never hear Father-in-law jokes and women always are made to look smarter than the men?

Have you ever noticed ...

A man gets upset when his date knows more about sports than he does?

Have you ever noticed ...

Men will complain about how hard their jobs are and never consider how hard their wife is working?

Have you ever noticed ...

When you stare at a girl wearing a very short skirt, she gets mad at you for staring?

Have you ever noticed ...

When men are driving by themselves, they don't often encounter any problems, but when their wife is with them there is always something he does when driving that happens that gets her upset?

Have you ever noticed ...

People who don't read newspapers, magazines or books hardly ever have much to say other than how things went at work?

Have you ever noticed ...

That a person who doesn't like your choice of music, or the books you read, or the TV shows you watch, may not be the person for you to date?

Have you ever noticed ...

A girl can have 100 pair of earrings but not one pair matches the outfit she wants to wear?

Have you ever noticed ...

Men and women put a roll of toilet paper on the holder differently? Women let the beginning hang down the back while men let it fall down the front.

Have you ever noticed ...
Women want to be treated as equals until it comes to killing a spider?

Have you ever noticed ...
More women are getting tattoos, but few of them say that they love a special guy, where a man will have a tattoo with the name or picture of a woman?

Have you ever noticed ...
When a man gets sick, his wife is there to take care of him just like a baby, but let the wife get sick and she's left to take care of herself?

Have you ever noticed ...
It is usually the woman that chooses the color of the car?

Have you ever noticed ...
When you tell your wife/husband that you love them they will always smile and tell you that they love you too?

Have you ever noticed ...
How you complain about your wife or husbands driving and it's you that gets the ticket?

Have you ever noticed ...
That you can bring a man's shirt and a woman's blouse to a cleaners and the man's shirt will always be less expensive to clean even though the material on both garments are the same?

Have you ever noticed ...
Your best rebuttal thoughts come to you two hours after the end of the argument?

Have you ever noticed ...
Women wear high heel shoes and then complain that their feet hurt?

Have you ever noticed ...
New women's hairdos look like they just got out of bed?

Have you ever noticed ...
Sitting on a bus, an elderly person gets on, and there are no seats, it takes a while before a man would offer his seat, but women would do so first?

Have you ever noticed ...
Women no longer wear girdles and it shows?

Have you ever noticed...

People constantly go to the refrigerator with the hope that something new to eat will have materialized?

Have you ever noticed ...

Men will delay doing any home repairs because it's raining, but that doesn't bother them if they want to play a round of golf?

Have you ever noticed ...

That before a man marries; he will bring his girl friend flowers and gifts? Then why does she ask what he's done wrong when he brings her flowers and gifts after their married?

Have you ever noticed...
That statistics on sanity are that one out of every four persons is suffering from some sort of mental illness? You're convinced that your husband/wife thinks it's you!

Have you ever noticed...
When waking up during the middle of the night and find that your husband/wife was watching TV, they will immediately ask, "Did I wake you up?"

Have you ever noticed...
Should your husband/wife go to the bathroom during the middle of the night, and being very careful not to make any noise, you will wake up anyway?

Have you ever noticed...

While watching a football game on TV, your wife will ask you, "what inning are they in?"

Have You Ever Noticed

People Are People

Have you ever noticed ...

How happy parents are at the engagement of a child over 40?

Have you ever noticed ...

When two or more ex-servicemen get together their conversation always goes toward their experiences in the service?

Have you ever noticed ...

That some dogs that hate to have someone blow in their face will put their heads out the car window for the entire ride?

Have you ever noticed ...

When you say "thank you" a person's face will light up?

Have you ever noticed ...

People who demand most of your time are unwilling to give you any of their time?

Have you ever noticed ...

That as soon as you do one special favor for someone, they will immediately ask you for another?

Have you ever noticed ...
When you ask people how they feel, they will actually tell you?

Have you ever noticed ...
People who sell raffle tickets always try to get you to buy more than you really want, and make you feel badley if you don't buy any at all?

Have you ever noticed ...
People who have had no business experience are always the ones to give advice on business?

Have you ever noticed ...

That the same people who cancel plans at the last moment without feeling guilt are the ones who are the most upset when others cancel plans with them?

Have you ever noticed ...

That women fashion seems to change 10 times a year while men's fashion seems to change once every 10 years?

Have you ever noticed ...

People who own dogs or cats will kiss them and the animals will kiss back, then the person wants to give you a kiss and you turn your face?

Have you ever noticed ...
That if it weren't for the cash register that automatically figures out how much change is to be given, that some register clerks would be unable to do their job?

Have you ever noticed ...
How many people no longer have home phones and only use their cell phones; and how annoying it is every time they fade in and out?

Have you ever noticed ...
When out to eat in a restaurant, that no matter how old they are, women have to go to the bathroom together?

Have you ever noticed ...
That people who tell ethnic jokes get upset if you tell jokes about their ethnic background?

Have you ever noticed ...
When a couple want to buy someone else's property, they feel that they should be given a better deal because they are nice, but when they want to sell they feel that they're entitled to every dime?

Have you ever noticed ...
When something your repairing goes wrong, no matter how hard you try, it continues to go wrong?

Have you ever noticed ...

When inviting friends for dinner the guests almost always bring a bottle of wine, but the host just never opens it for dinner?

Have you ever noticed ...

How many times at a party someone would say "excuse me for a minute", leave the conversation and never return?

Have you ever noticed ...

That people seem to speak louder if they think the person they're talking to doesn't understand their language?

Have you ever noticed ...
That some people in order to avoid a charitable contribution say they can't afford to do so, but claim the deduction on their income taxes anyway?

Have you ever noticed ...
That no matter how sound asleep you are, you still hear your husband/wife get up to go to the bathroom at night?

Have you ever noticed ...
That if you smile at someone who has been screaming at you that they just get madder and you feel better?

Have you ever noticed ...

That years ago a girl would die before letting anyone see her "bra" straps and today it's part of the look?

Have you ever noticed ...

That some people that can barely walk to the car are the ones driving it? Now do you feel any safer driving on the same road?

Have you ever noticed ...

How many people have to endure difficult people to reach their goals, and when they do so become "difficult", making it hard for someone else?

Have you ever noticed …
Young people will not take the same advice now that they will be giving to their children later on?

Have you ever noticed …
Some people say that they're not prejudiced and then proceed to open their mouths and prove that they are?

Have you ever noticed …
When someone is making a major purchase they always bring a friend along for advice – a friend, who can't afford to buy the item, and will find every reason for the buyer not do so?

Have you ever noticed ...

When someone is given too much change, for the most part they will keep it and say nothing, but if they are not given the correct amount they make a major case out of the mistake?

Have you ever noticed ...

That you can remember the name of the person who influenced you the most even if it happened when you were a child?

Have you ever noticed ...

Some people who never show up on time get mad at you for complaining, and don't understand what they've done wrong, and why you are upset?

Have you ever noticed ...
Someone else's pet will always want to be petted by some one who doesn't like pets?

Have you ever noticed ...
That you can proofread a letter a hundred times, send it out and only then notice a misspelling?

Have you ever noticed ...
That people who leave the toilet seat up never read books?

Have you ever noticed ...
You still call a "CD" a record and forget the difference between "CD" and "DVD?"

Have you ever noticed ...
Over weight people say they're doing everything possible to lose weight while putting on extra dressing over their salad?

Have you ever noticed ...
How good you feel when you tell someone your age and they immediately say "you look so much younger?"

Have you ever noticed ...

That people who say your doing something wrong, never stay around long enough to say how to do it right?

Have you ever noticed ...

That there are a great number of people who always say, "that can't be done," and before you can respond someone has already done it?

Have you ever noticed ...

When you're out to lunch with someone who thinks that you are better off, financially, will seldom offer to pick up the check?

Have you ever noticed ...
The person in school elected "most likely to succeed," doesn't, and the person thought least likely to succeed, does?

Have you ever noticed ...
That some manicurists really don't have pretty nails?

Have you ever noticed ...
How many people judge others by the way they look, rather than first talking to them and knowing who they really are?

Have you ever noticed ...
When you're in a hurry you always hit the red lights, and when you have time you always make the green ones?

Have you ever noticed ...
Just when you're ready to get on the phone, have a business meeting, or want to take a nap, that's when the gardener starts the blower?

Have you ever noticed ...
It's the rich that argue over the pennies and seldom worry about the dollars?

Have you ever noticed ...

When you say, "I have something to tell you, but don't get mad at me", and they say they wouldn't, but they always do?

Have you ever noticed ...

When you ask, out of politeness, "How are you?" many will proceed to tell you, and tell you, and tell you?

Have you ever noticed ...

The great idea you had last night was completely forgotten when you woke up the following morning?

Have you ever noticed ...
Once you've lent a friend money, they soon forget that they were your friend and also forget about the loan?

Have you ever noticed ...
That people selling items at a garage sale get offended when receiving a low offer? Isn't that better than no offer at all? Isn't a low offer a good starting place to find out what the seller really wants?

Have you ever noticed ...
That slow drivers are always in the fast lane and only move over to your lane when your trying to get around them?

Have you ever noticed ...

How good you feel when one of your children/grand children call you up just to say they love you?

Have you ever noticed ...

How nice a police officer is, even when giving you a ticket?

Have you ever noticed ...

That the person who complains the most also creates most of the problems?

Have you ever noticed ...

That people who served in the military stand straighter?

Have you ever noticed ...

That, after a while people begin to look likes their pets?

Have you ever noticed ...

That people don't install an alarm system on their home until after they've been broken into?

Have you ever noticed ...

During the winter, people who live in the warm area of the country will call their friends on the East Coast just to tell them how warm it is?

Have you ever noticed ...

Boxes of Girl Scout cookies are getting smaller?

Have you ever noticed ...

That after an argument, and you're by yourself, you can think of all the things you really wanted to say and have all the right answers to the questions thrown at you during the argument?

Have you ever noticed ...
How some people will drive slow in the fast lane and get upset when you try to go around them?

Have you ever noticed ...
That some people will ask a favor, and when you agree to do the favor (after much difficulty) the person will cancel and think nothing of the problems they have put you through?

Have you ever noticed ...
That the person, who consistently uses foul language, has a very small vocabulary?

Have you ever noticed ...
That people who have very little knowledge of a subject always have a great deal to say about it?

Have you ever noticed ...
That some people wear the most awful, outlandish clothes, and when you stare at them they get upset?

Have you ever noticed ...
That when you need a pen and a piece of paper there is none to be found, but when you don't need either they're all over the place?

Have you ever noticed ...

When friends hear that you're thinking of purchasing a new home, get personal and ask you financial questions that they would never have done so before?

Have you ever noticed ...

People who make promises have short memories?

Have you ever noticed ...

That a person who yells and carries on a lot will always mellow when he's spoken to softly and given lots of compliments?

Have you ever noticed ...

That once an error appears on important documents that no matter how hard you try to make corrections the problem just gets worse?

Have you ever noticed ...

That most people look better with their clothes on than off?

Have you ever noticed ...

That blackjack dealers can only count to 21 and get stuck on 17?

Have you ever noticed ...

That a person says their complaint is not about money, but after telling you about their complaint you find out that it is about money?

Have you ever noticed ...

How you feel when the holiday bills start coming in?

Have you ever noticed ...

People who have a chip on their shoulder will do everything possible to add another one as well?

Have you ever noticed ...

That the instructions given to hang wallpaper seem so easy, but doing it turns out to be harder than expected?

Have you ever noticed ...

That after reading the instructions for the new digital camera, you wonder why you bought it in the first place?

Have you ever noticed ...

People who will not bend on anything will say that they're the most flexible people around?

Have you ever noticed ...

The person you have the most respect for will never disappoint you even if he/she doesn't know of your feelings?

Have you ever noticed ...

That small dogs bark more and louder than big dogs and they are more aggressive than big dogs?

Have you ever noticed ...

That the person you thought was your friend really wasn't and the person you thought was an acquaintance turns out to be a real friend?

Have you ever noticed ...

People who question your comments are, most likely, the same people whose comments you question?

Have you ever noticed ...

That it's much more difficult writing about your thoughts than just talking about them?

Have you ever noticed ...

That the older you get the faster time seems to go?

Have you ever noticed ...

That people who give you advice on buying or not to buy are the same people who can't buy anything?

Have you ever noticed ...

When speaking softly and politely you can get a service agency to take care of your problem sooner than by yelling and carrying on?

Have you ever noticed ...

When telling someone that you're writing a book they will say, "Really?"

Have you ever noticed ...
When receiving a letter from the IRS that you become very nervous before even opening the envelope?

Have you ever noticed ...
That the person who won the raffle, usually bought only one ticket?

Have you ever noticed ...
That some graffiti painters really have artistic talent? They also seem to get into places that most people would never attempt, and they don't clean up after themselves.

Have you ever noticed ...

After your house has been painted and the painter leaves, you find a spot that he missed?

Have you ever noticed ...

That upon seeing a police car you will automatically drive at the posted speed limit and once the police car turns off you go faster?

Have you ever noticed ...

Telemarketers will hang up on you if you ask for their phone number and name?

Have you ever noticed ...

That speaking very softly, you can get an angry person to speak to you in a more pleasant tone?
(Saying this twice so you wouldn't forget)

Have you ever noticed ...

That you can hear two men of the cloth speak from the same page in the Bible and give you two different meanings?

Have you ever noticed ...

A person who just bought a five year old car will tell everyone that he/she just got a new car?

Have you ever noticed ...

Shoes will feel great when trying them on in the store, but when you wear them the next day, they feel tight?

Have you ever noticed ...

Successful people will always thank someone for leading them in the right direction or helping them along the way. People, who think they did it all by themselves, just don't want to admit they had help.

Have you ever noticed ...

That you hardly ever see a white horse run at a racetrack yet all of the cowboys' horses were white and they all ran like the wild wind? (For my wife, "white" and "gray" are different colors)

Have you ever noticed ...

When it's really warm you want the weather to cool down and when it does, you then want the warm weather to return?

Have you ever noticed ...

When you get your car washed, later that day it rains?

Have you ever noticed ...

The day you finally decide to get your haircut, it looks better than it has in weeks?

Have you ever noticed ...

Whenever you do a "big" food shopping and you buy all the ingredients for your favorite meal, you're too worn out to cook anything that evening?

Have you ever noticed ...

That as soon as you get into the shower, the phone rings?

Have you ever noticed ...

No matter how many pairs of reading glasses you have, there is never a pair close by?

Have you ever noticed ...

On the mornings you decide to stay in your robe a little longer, that's when unexpected company arrives?

Have you ever noticed ...

On those days you don't look your best, you run into a lot of people that you haven't seen in awhile?

Have you ever noticed ...

That when a person is given an opportunity of doing the right thing, they will?

Have you ever noticed ...
People will stop in front of a doorway or isle to talk to someone and block anyone from getting around them?

Have you ever noticed ...
An accident caused by some one who has had too much to drink, normally ends up with the innocent person being hurt and the drunk walking away without a scratch?

Have you ever noticed ...
A person who is always running late will tell you that they'll be ready in "just a minute?"

Have you ever noticed ...

After a person tells you their age and you say that they look much younger, that they smile for the rest of the day?

Have you ever noticed ...

When a small child wants you to watch what they're doing they'll take you by the hand and lead you to where they want you to sit? Now, isn't that wonderful?

Have you ever noticed ...

After going up to the highest floor in a very high building that you don't want to look out the window because of the height?

Have you ever noticed ...

(For the guys) when your wife says she deserves a medal for being married to you, and you give her one, that she will actually be proud to wear it?

I know from experience, as I gave my wife two medals, ten years apart, and they're still not big enough!

Have you ever noticed ...

That 50 years ago your parents begged you to cut your hair, and today you wished you had hair to cut?

Have you ever noticed ...

How ill you got when you were sent to the principal's office and how ill you now get when your kid is in the principal's office?

Have you ever noticed ...

We don't have wax paper anymore, kids no longer paper bag their lunches and we never worried about E. coli and we seemed to live through it all without any worry or complaint?

Have you ever noticed ...

You've only had your new car a couple of weeks, and were very careful where you parked it – away from everyone else – and one day you discover someone scratched it and from that point on you didn't care where you parked the car?

Have you ever noticed ...

You don't hear yourself snore?

Have you ever noticed ...
When deciding not to purchase something that you really, really want until the price comes down and when it does, someone else got there first and purchased it?

Have you ever noticed...
You try running over a piece of string a dozen times with the vacuum cleaner, then reach down, pick it up, examine it, then put it down to give the vacuum one more chance?

Have you ever noticed...
That you can only remember a small portion of your dreams and never how it ends?

Have you ever noticed...

You would never think twice about losing $100.00 at a casino, but you get upset at having to pay $100.00 for the dentist?

About Real Estate

Have you ever noticed ...

When your not dressed at your best and driving the family truck and you want to see a very expensive property that the real estate agent says they have another appointment and will find someone else to take you out?

Have you ever noticed ...

When you come to the real estate office and you had no choice but to bring the kids, the real estate agent doesn't look very happy?

Have you ever noticed ...

When the real estate agent is driving a nicer car than you, you feel intimidated?

Have you ever noticed ...

When you tell the real estate agent that you don't want to spend over $200,000, need at least 4 bedrooms and four baths, that there must be a pool; that the agent will just stare with open mouth and not able to say anything?

Have you ever noticed ...

When the real estate agent says that they're number one in sales and you say that you don't want to spend much, that they let their assistant show you property?

Have you ever noticed ...

The expression on the Realtors® face when you kiddingly say, "You mean I have to make a down payment?"

Have you ever noticed ...

When the advertising says that the views are great, you discover that the views can only be seen by standing along the side of the house?

Have you ever noticed ...

When the advertising says that there's plenty of room for a pool and spa that there is no way to get into the yard for the contractor to dig the pool and spa?

Have you ever noticed ...

When the advertising says, "Golf within a few minute drive," that all of those courses require membership and the cost is more than the house you're thinking of buying?

Have you ever noticed ...

When you tell a friend that you are going to look for a new home, they immediately say they have a friend who is a Realtor®; you then find out that the friend just got their license and hasn't the slightest idea where to start?

Have you ever noticed ...

When being shown a property in a gated community and there are security guards, you wonder if there is a crime problem?

Have you ever noticed ...

When you don't ask questions, that you get the same number of answers?

Have you ever noticed ...

When friends brag that they bought a condo for $150,000 and then sold it for $200,000, making a $50,000 profit that they forgot to say that after paying buyers and sellers commissions, escrow costs, state tax and 35 percent to the IRS for short term gains, that the actual profit was nothing?

Have you ever noticed ...

When you have a high "FICO score, you get a lower interest rate and if you don't have a good score you pay a higher interest rate. Do you ever wonder if that's right?

Have you ever noticed ...

Lenders will talk about "FICO" scores but never explain what they are, just as I am now doing?

Have You Ever Noticed

Some Late Comers

Have you ever noticed ...

When a man is driving to a never before visited place, that his wife will say he's going the wrong way and she'll feel very happy and smug to know that she was right?

Have you ever noticed ...

That blockbuster movie will be available on DVD after a very short time of being released in the theaters and will cost less to purchase than to watch in a theater, yet you still will go to the theater to see it?

Have you ever noticed ...

People will say that I'm going to spend my two-week vacation just sleeping, eating and reading but after the first day or two they're antsy and want to do something or go somewhere?

Have you ever noticed ...

You can repeat a comedians joke word for word, yet it will never sound the same nor get the same response?

Have you ever noticed ...

That credit card companies are not satisfied with how much you charge each month and now have advertising
Flyers inserted with your invoices with the hope that you will spend more?

Have you ever noticed ...

That men and women are different in the morning? Upon wakening men will get up and go to the bathroom and upon returning the wife will ask him to bring her a cup of coffee and he then brags that he brings his wife breakfast in the morning?

Have you ever noticed ...
When a woman is pregnant and she feels the baby kicking, she'll say, "Oh my god, he's kicking. Do you "wanna" feel it?"

Have you ever noticed ...
After reading this book that you have items that you think should be in the book?

Have you ever noticed ...
Parents got very concerned when their daughter brought home a young man with tattoos and pins through his ears, lips and nose, now the parents get concerned when the "son" brings home a girl with tattoos and pins through her ears, lips and nose?

Have you ever noticed...

When an older person gets into an accident, the newspaper will always print the elder persons age, but never prints the age of a younger person who gets into an accident?

Have you ever noticed...

If you take the first letters of North, East, West and South, that it spells "NEWS?" By the way, that's how we got the word.

Have you ever noticed...

That the casino says that they have plenty of 1-Cent (penny) slot machines, but the least amount that you can play is $0.25 cents?

Have You Ever Noticed

Be sure to read all of the fine books written by Louis Perlin:

Just Ask Lou!

Over 250 questions and most important, the answers you need to know before your next real estate transaction.

* * * * *

Just Ask Lou... Some More!

A series of important articles that address every aspect of modern Real Estate.

* * * * *

To contact Mr. Perlin write to:
453 E. Tahquitz Canyon Way
Palm Springs, California 92262
Or,
Call: (760) 327-8401
FAX: (769) 327-7651

Look for these and other fine books from:

Williams Publishing
6176 Driver Road
Palm Springs, California 92264
(760) 902-1972
Or visit our website at:
www.wmpbooks.com